Jesus and the Miracle

This

Bible Story Time book

belongs to

JOShua+

Adam.

Text by Sophie Piper
Illustrations copyright © 2006 Estelle Corke
This edition copyright © 2014 Lion Hudson

Published by Lion Children's Books
an imprint of
Lion Hudson plc
Wilkinson House, Jordan Hill Road,
Oxford OX2 8DR, England
www.lionhudson.com/lionchildrens

ISBN 978 0 7459 6361 7
e-ISBN 978 0 7459 6814 8

First edition 2006
This edition 2014

A catalogue record for this book is available from the British Library

Printed and bound in China, October 2013, LH06

Jesus and the Miracle

Sophie Piper ✳ Estelle Corke

LION
CHILDREN'S

One day, Jesus went to the town of Capernaum. The news spread quickly.

"Look – Jesus is here! He's staying at the same house as before. All kinds of people are going to hear him speak."

"Hurry! There won't be much room left."

A mother and her daughter watched as the crowds hurried by.

"Why are those men carrying that man down the street on his mattress?" asked the little girl.

"The poor man cannot walk," replied her mother. "But I wonder where they are taking him?"

"Oh! I think I can guess!"

"They want to see Jesus. Look at the crowds who have come to see him!"

"Everyone says that Jesus can work miracles," said the little girl's mother. "I think the men want Jesus to heal their friend."

"But how can they get to Jesus?" asked the little girl. "The house is crowded. No one wants to let them in."

The four men were puzzled too.

"We can't get in the door," said one.

"We can't get NEAR the door," said the second.

"And those steps only go to the roof," said the third.

"LET'S GO TO THE ROOF!" said the fourth.

The roof was flat. The men started digging into it.

"What's the plan?" asked the man on the mattress.

"The plan is to take you to Jesus," said the friends.

Soon they had dug deep into the roof.

One of the men fetched some rope.
They tied a length to each corner
of the mattress.

"Now we must do the last bit
quickly," said another of the men.
"Ready – GO!"

They made the hole go right
through the ceiling.

They lowered their friend down
on his mattress.

"I can see people smiling..." said
one of the men on the roof.

"I don't see everybody smiling,"
said another.

Jesus spoke to the man on the bed.
"Your sins are forgiven," he said.
  The people next to Jesus began
to whisper.

  "Did you hear? Jesus said the man
was forgiven for all the bad things
he has ever done."

  "Tut, tut. Only God can forgive
like that."

  "Jesus isn't a proper teacher.
We're proper teachers. We know
what's right."

19

Jesus looked at the teachers.

"I know what you're thinking," he said.

"You don't like me saying, 'Your sins are forgiven.' But I'm going to show you something. What I say really is what God wants to say."

He turned to the man on the bed.
"Get up, pick up your bed, and go
home!"

The man on the bed could see Jesus'
kind face.
  He could see the teachers frowning.
  He could see his friends waving
down to him.
  He knew he must try to sit up.

He did sit up.

He stood up.

He took a step. Then he danced a little jig around the mattress!

He bent down and rolled the mattress into a bundle.

"See you outside," called his friends.

"Thank you, God! Thank you, Jesus! Thank you, friends!" the man was singing.

"Hooray! Hooray!" cried his friends.

"Look," said the little girl to her mother. "The man is carrying his mattress now. He can walk very well."

"So Jesus really can heal people,"
said her mother. "No wonder they
believe he is God's Son."